Designer Dogs

Goldendoodles

by Ruth Owen

PowerKiDS
press.

New York

Published in 2013 by The Rosen Publishing Group, Inc.
29 East 21st Street, New York, NY 10010

First Edition

Produced for Rosen by Ruby Tuesday Books Ltd
Editor for Ruby Tuesday Books Ltd: Mark J. Sachner
US Editor: Sara Antill
Designer: Emma Randall

Photo Credits:

Cover, 1, 3, 4–5, 6–7, 8–9, 10–11, 12–13, 15, 19, 29, 30 © Shutterstock; 14 © Corbis; 16 © Superstock; 17 © Istock; 21, 22 © Miguel Ola and Judi Gomez; 23 © Guide Dogs of America; 24–25 © Glenene Brown; 26–27 © Paulette Gooder, American Search Dogs.

Library of Congress Cataloging-in-Publication Data

Owen, Ruth, 1967–
 Goldendoodles / by Ruth Owen. — 1st ed.
    p. cm. — (Designer dogs)
 Includes index.
 ISBN 978-1-4488-7856-7 (library binding) — ISBN 978-1-4488-7909-0 (pbk.)
 — ISBN 978-1-4488-7915-1 (6-pack)
 1. Goldendoodle—Juvenile literature. I. Title.
 SF429.G64O94 2013
 636.72—dc23

                                    2012001536

Manufactured in the United States of America

CPSIA Compliance Information: Batch #B1S12PK: For Further Information contact Rosen Publishing, New York, New York at 1-800-237-9932

Contents

woof

Meet a Goldendoodle

What is friendly, very smart, and has curly hair? The answer is a goldendoodle.

Goldendoodles are a type of **crossbreed** dog. This means they are a mixture of two different dog **breeds**, or types. When a golden retriever and a poodle have puppies together, they make goldendoodles!

Most goldendoodles are family pets, but some have been trained to work as **search and rescue dogs** and **guide dogs**.

Adult golden retriever

Adult poodle

Goldendoodle puppy

A goldendoodle

Goldendoodles are also known as goldenpoos, goldie poos, and groodles.

5

Designer Doodles

Many people love dogs but have an **allergy** to their hair and skin. If an allergic person gets close to a dog, that person may start sneezing or have trouble breathing.

Poodles have hair that does not make allergic people ill. So, some **dog breeders** decided to mix poodles with other dog breeds.

One new breed that was created in the 1990s was a large, intelligent, retriever-like dog with poodle-like hair called a goldendoodle. Many people with a dog allergy do not get sick when they are around a goldendoodle!

Goldendoodles and other crossbreeds, such as labradoodles and schnoodles, are often called "designer dogs." This is because dog breeders designed, or created, them.

A labradoodle is created from a Labrador retriever and a poodle.

A schnoodle is created from a schnauzer and a poodle.

Meet the Parents: Golden Retrievers

Golden retrievers were first bred in Scotland, in the 1800s, to be gun dogs. When their owners were shooting birds, such as pheasants or ducks, the dogs would retrieve the dead birds and bring them back to the hunters.

Today, many golden retrievers still work as gun dogs. They also work as guide dogs or as detectors of **illegal drugs** at airports. They sniff passengers' luggage to check if people are carrying drugs.

Adult golden retriever size

Height to shoulder = up to 24 inches (61 cm)

Golden retrievers are very popular as family pets. They are gentle, intelligent dogs that love to please their owners.

A golden retriever retrieving a bird

Golden retriever puppies

Meet the Parents: Poodles

Poodles are good swimmers, and they love to be in water. They were originally bred to help people hunt ducks and other water birds. When a hunter shot a bird, the poodle retrieved it from the water and carried it back to its master.

Sometimes people clip, or cut, a poodle's coat. Poodles were first given haircuts to help them move through water more easily. Some hair was left to keep the dog's joints and organs, such as its lungs, warm in cold water.

Adult standard poodle size

A clipped poodle with a corded coat

Height to shoulder = over 15 inches (38 cm)

Poodles may have woolly or **corded** coats. Poodles come in many different sizes, from tiny toy poodles to large standard poodles.

A clipped poodle with a curly coat

Gorgeous Goldendoodles

A goldendoodle may have a shaggy coat, like its golden retriever parent, a curly coat like a poodle, or something in between. The hair can grow as long as 8 inches (20 cm). Goldendoodles need to be groomed every few weeks.

A goldendoodle's coat may be a shade of gold or a poodle color such as cream, apricot, chocolate, black, or even silver.

Adult goldendoodle size

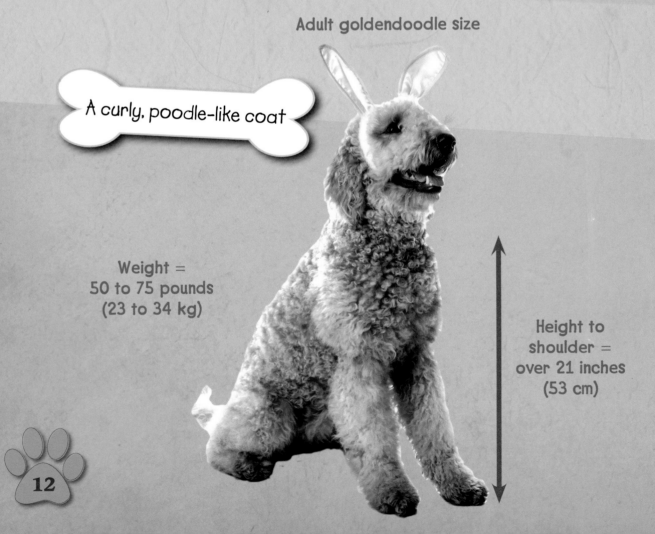

A curly, poodle-like coat

Weight =
50 to 75 pounds
(23 to 34 kg)

Height to
shoulder =
over 21 inches
(53 cm)

12

A shaggy, retriever-like coat

Goldendoodles can live to be about 15 years old.

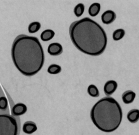

Goldendoodle Personalities

Like their parent breeds, goldendoodles are very smart and love to be taught new things. They also like to make new friends with strangers, other dogs, and other pet animals.

Goldendoodles **bond** strongly with their human family. These gentle, easygoing dogs are happy living in a city apartment or on a farm, just as long as they have people around them.

If a goldendoodle is left home alone all day, it may become unhappy. Then the bored, lonely pup may get into mischief!

Everyone is a goldendoodle's friend—even the vet!

Goldendoodle Puppies

A goldendoodle puppy normally has a golden retriever mom and a poodle dad. The mom dog usually gives birth to a **litter** of eight to ten puppies.

The newborn puppies drink milk from their mom. They sleep cuddled up with their brothers and sisters.

By the time they are four weeks old, the puppies are running around and playing. At eight to ten weeks old, they are big enough to leave their mom and go to live with their new human family.

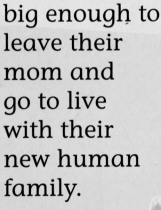

Seven-week-old goldendoodle puppies

Sometimes a goldendoodle litter may be as large as 14 or 16 puppies!

Goldendoodle pups love to make new friends!

Goldendoodles Love to Help

Some goldendoodle puppies are chosen to do very special jobs.

Because goldendoodles are quick to learn new things, friendly, and eager to please, they can be trained to help people.

Hearing assist dogs help people who are deaf. The dogs are trained to listen for sounds such as the doorbell, a smoke detector, or an oven timer. Then they lead their owner to the sound.

Service dogs work with people who use a wheelchair or have other disabilities. The dogs turn lights on and off and pick up objects that their owners drop.

Richter: A Very Special Puppy

Richter the goldendoodle was the world's first goldendoodle guide dog.

When Richter was eight weeks old, he was given to the Guide Dogs of America organization by his breeder. He went to live with a puppy raiser named Judith. It was Judith's job to teach Richter how to sit, stay, lie down, and walk on a leash. She also took Richter to work and busy places, such as malls, to help him get used to people and noises.

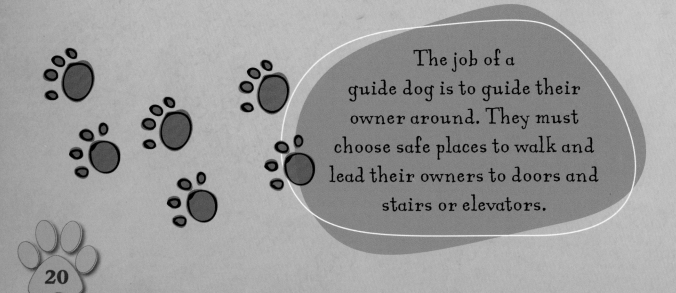

The job of a guide dog is to guide their owner around. They must choose safe places to walk and lead their owners to doors and stairs or elevators.

Richter at two
months old

21

Richter: The Goldendoodle Guide Dog

Richter did well at his puppy training. When he was 18 months old, he began working with a trainer from Guide Dogs of America.

Richter learned to stop at roadside curbs and at the top and bottom of stairs. He learned how to lead a person onto buses and trains, and how to steer them away from danger, such as holes in the street.

On May 1, 2005, Richter graduated as a guide dog!

Richter training to be a guide dog

Richter now enjoys his busy life as a guide dog, helping his owner Melissa, who is blind.

Richter wearing his guide dog harness

Rufus: The Therapy Goldendoodle

Rufus the therapy dog has been trained to visit people who are in the hospital. Rufus's job is to comfort people who are sick and cheer them up! When visiting children, Rufus often sits on their beds to be petted.

People who have been injured might need to do exercises to help their bodies recover. Brushing Rufus or throwing treats for him is good exercise, and it's fun!

To cheer up hospital patients on the holidays, Rufus wears costumes!

When a child was learning to use artificial legs, Rufus was there to help. He walked up and down the hospital corridors with the little boy.

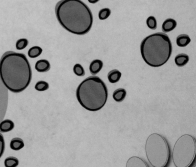

Murphy: Search and Rescue Dog

Murphy the goldendoodle and his owner Paulette work as part of a search and rescue team. Murphy has been trained to use his powerful sense of smell to find people who are lost.

If a child is lost in a forest, Murphy is given a piece of the child's clothing to smell. He knows to search only for that scent.

In the forest, Murphy quickly moves ahead of Paulette, sniffing. He may pick up a scent where the child walked. If Murphy finds the child, he runs to Paulette and leads her to the child!

Murphy and Paulette

Sometimes Murphy searches lakes or rivers for a person who has drowned. He rides in a boat and sniffs the water. His powerful nose can pick up the scent of a body, even when it is underwater.

Run, Dozer, Run!

What can a goldendoodle do to burn off energy? He can become a **marathon** runner!

In 2011, Dozer the goldendoodle was in his yard. Passing by his house were hundreds of runners taking part in the University of Maryland's 13-mile (21-km) half marathon. Dozer escaped from his garden, joined the race, and even crossed the finish line!

Dozer returned home the next day limping and with muddy paws. When his owners heard stories of a marathon-running dog, they realized it was Dozer.

Dozer was presented with a medal for finishing the race!

The University of Maryland half marathon is run to raise money for a cancer charity. Dozer wasn't sponsored when he ran the race, but an online page was set up in his name so people could donate money!

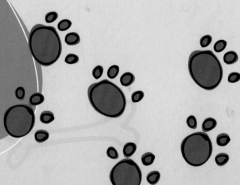

Glossary

allergy (A-lur-jee) When a person's body reacts badly to something such as an animal or type of food. An allergy may make a person sneeze, get sore skin, vomit, or become seriously ill.

bond (BOND) To form a close connection based on love and trust.

breed (BREED) A type of dog. Also, the word used to describe the act of mating two dogs in order for them to have puppies.

corded (KORD-ed) Having long, tightly curled strands of hair, somewhat like dreadlocks.

crossbreed (KROS-breed) A type of dog created from two different breeds.

dog breeder (DAWG BREED-er) A person who breeds dogs and sells them.

guide dog (GYD DAWG) A dog that is trained to lead and protect a person who is blind or has difficulty seeing.

illegal drug (ih-LEE-gul DRUG) A type of drug that is against the law to use or sell.

litter (LIH-ter) A group of baby animals all born to the same mother at the same time.

marathon (MAR-uh-thon) A race that is just over 26 miles (42 km) long and is usually run on roads.

search and rescue dog (SERCH AND RES-kyoo DAWG) A dog trained to use its sense of smell to search for lost people.

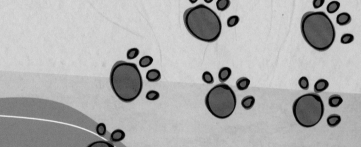

Websites

Due to the changing nature of Internet links, PowerKids Press has developed an online list of websites related to the subject of this book. This site is updated regularly. Please use this link to access the list:

www.powerkidslinks.com/ddog/golden/

Read More

George, Charles, and Linda George. *Golden Retriever.* Top Dogs. New York: Scholastic, 2010.

Landau, Elaine. *Poodles Are the Best!* Best Dogs Ever. Minneapolis, MN: Lerner Publications, 2010.

Wheeler, Jill C. *Goldendoodles.* Minneapolis, MN: Checkerboard Books, 2008.

Index